What Leaders Need
to Know and Do

A Leadership Competencies Scorecard

Brent D. Ruben, Ph.D.

For information on the use of the LCSI program or materials contact: Dr. Brent D. Ruben, Executive Director, Center for Organizational Development and Leadership, 4 Huntington Street, Rutgers, The State University of New Jersey, New Brunswick, NJ 08901-1071. Voice: 732/932-1420; Fax: 732/932-1422; E-mail: ruben@odl.rutgers.edu.

Library of Congress Cataloging-in-Publication Data

Ruben, Brent D.
  What leaders need to know and do: A leadership competencies scorecard / Brent D. Ruben.
     p. cm.
  Includes bibliographical references.
  ISBN-13: 978-1-56972-038-7
  1. Leadership--Evaluation. I. National Association of College and University Business Officers. II. Title.
  HM1261.R83 2006
  658.4'092--dc22

                         2006010747

Design by Colburnhouse

National Association of College and University Business Officers
Washington, DC
www.nacubo.org

Printed in the United States of America

Contents

Acknowledgments

I began the research upon which this book is based while on sabbatical two years ago. Surveying the academic, professional, and popular literature required the concentrated period of time that the sabbatical afforded, and I am indebted to Rutgers for making the research leave possible.

The ideas that come together in a project such as this are never solely one's own. I am grateful to friends and colleagues at Rutgers and other institutions and organizations with whom I have conversed about leadership in various contexts over the years. For their contributions to my thinking and their encouragement to write this book, I am most grateful.

Preface

I have long been fascinated by the topic of leadership and have come to regard it as one of the most important variables in social life. Whether one thinks of decision making within a family or group of friends, formalized assessment and strategic planning processes within a large organization, or policy making and diplomatic activity at the level of national or international politics, leadership dynamics are at work in crucial ways.

So often, when one hears that a group or organization is being recognized for particular accomplishments, a close examination reveals that much of the credit lies with the leadership. The people who lead such groups and organizations to distinction do not always have a flashy or flamboyant style. In many instances, those who provide important leadership functions do not even occupy formal positions of authority; rather they make their contributions subtly through informal interpersonal communication and personal influence. I have observed, also, that leaders who have a major impact on those around them are not always publicly revered and celebrated; to the extent that their work is noticed, the benefits of their leadership may be visible primarily in the leadership team or culture they create, or in the results they achieve. And those may become apparent only years later—or not at all.

Two Parables

The ways in which we think about leadership can have a profound consequences for human affairs—consequences which may be revealed as much by cartoonists and comedians, as by biographers and eminent researchers. While I don't purport to be any of these, I do want to offer readers of this Preface two parables. I believe each captures in satirical form a number of foundational issues of significance in contemporary leadership theory and practice.

The Little Train That Could: The Untold Story

Once upon a time there was a little train filled with toys and animals, new cars, TVs and all kinds of stuff, and people—headed down the track on its way to the city. It was a long train with a shiny silver engine up front, and some freight cars, a passenger car, and a red caboose at the end.

The Engine had a bright light, a bell, and a horn. As it went down the track toward the city, the Engine rang its bell and honked its horn as it headed happily over hill and dale, proudly announcing its presence to everyone.

All was going well, until the train came to Mount Obstacle. As it headed into the upward grade, the train began to slow down a bit. The further up Obstacle it went, the slower its speed. Slower and slower it went.

The Engine looked ahead, and wondered to himself (most engines were men in those days) if he could make it. He knew how disappointed the people in the city would be if the train were delayed, and he also knew that the people and animals on the train were counting on him to be strong and steadfast.

He pondered the situation, and then began saying to himself, "I know I can, I know I can, I know I can." He talked to himself and kept his eyes fixed on the course ahead. He was proud, and he kept ringing the bell and honking the horn. But still the train slowed.

The Caboose and Passenger Car knew a problem existed and decided to try to get the Engine's attention to tell him they wanted to help and had some ideas. At first he didn't hear them because he was so preoccupied with Obstacle. Finally, the Engine heard their voices, but he couldn't stop the train to talk to them, so he honked the horn and waved the flag to acknowledge their support, and then blew smoke all over them thinking it might be best if he kept them in the "dark" about how he was going about surmounting Obstacle.

When the smoke cleared, the Passenger Car and the Caboose began to talk to each other. They talked about what they could do to help, and they came up with some good ideas. They talked about how to offer assistance in a way that the Engine would be able accept it. They knew they needed to lighten the load if the train was to make it over Obstacle, so they decided to throw off some extra empty boxes and other stuff they didn't need. (This was before the days of environmental awareness and recycling.) And they worked it out with the passengers so some got off and walked alongside the train to make it even lighter and others helped by pushing.

Suddenly, the train began to pick up speed. The Engine saw the improvement, and felt good. "I knew I could, I knew I could, I knew I could," he said to himself, and he rang the bell and honked the horn, and was very proud, as he made his way over the mountain and into the city right on time.

When the train came into the station, crowds were there waiting. They cheered and shouted, "We're glad you made it! We knew you could. We knew you would. You're the little Engine that could!"

The reporters interviewed the Engine, and the photographers took pictures. "Can you tell us how you feel about this achievement," a journalist asked.

"It took some extra effort, extra commitment, and extra conviction, but that's what being a leader is all about," the Engine responded, beaming with pride.

The people cheered, and the Engine beamed, and then everyone went home to live happily every after.

Several months later, a well-known author in the city decided he wanted to write a book about the train's achievements, and he began by interviewing the Engine.

The Engine was gracious and talked about the importance of commitment, high-energy leadership, and unwavering focus on the task at hand.

The author tried to find the Passenger Car and Caboose to interview them, but he learned that they had left town to hook up with a different train headed down a different track.

He finally located them and asked them to recall their experiences from the fateful day. "It was quite a day," the Passenger Car commented, as she recalled the lessons she had learned about collaboration and teamwork. The Caboose spoke of the importance of two-way communication, shared "ownership" of problems, and shared leadership.

"So, why did you leave?" the author asked.

"In the final analysis you could probably say it was the black smoke," the Caboose responded. "The Engine was always visible, out there shining his light, ringing his bell and honking his horn. And there we were—invisible, isolated, and in the dark.

The Passenger Car added, "It was okay being on the train, but I never really felt as though we were a part of the train."

Then the two commented in unison: "If you're writing a book about the events of that day, maybe you could title it *The Little Train That Could* rather than *The Little Engine That Could.*" Frankly, we've never really liked the original title all that much!

M. Peror's New Plan

Once upon a time, there lived a Director, M. Peror. Many employees, patrons, and visitors came each day to the great organization she led. One day, two consultants called on the Director. They said they were reorganization experts and declared they could develop the finest reorganization and change management plan anyone could imagine. They said their plans would be cutting edge, out-of-the-box, a new paradigm.

They explained that their plans possessed a wonderful additional quality—they were incomprehensible to anyone who was unfit for the position he or she held or was not visionary, effective, or fit as a leader.

"That would be a most excellent plan!" thought M. Peror. "If I put forth a plan developed by the consultants, I should be able to find out which men and women in my organization are unfit for the positions they hold; I could tell the visionary and effective ones from the unfit." And with that she hired the consultants and sent out an email to her colleagues explaining the project and the team's magical powers.

The consultants brought in their laptops and went to work. They requested extensive background materials, conducted focus groups, and interviewed many people. They had sophisticated graphics software and the most advanced overhead projection systems money could buy, and they worked on their computers until late into the night.

After a few weeks passed, the Director said to herself, "I would like to know how far they have progressed with the planning." She felt reluctant to meet with the consultants herself, recalling that those who were not fit for their offices could not understand it. She was confident, of course, that she had nothing to fear for herself, but she preferred to send someone else first to see how the work was coming along.

"I will send my valued Associate Director to the consultants," thought the Director. "He can judge best how the plan looks, for he has sense, and other than me, no one understands this organization's needs better than he." So the good Associate Director was dispatched to the office where the two rogues sat working at their computers.

"Mercy!" said the Associate Director. He gazed upon the documents, and thought to himself, "I see nothing here that is new or novel, or out-of-the-box, or paradigm-busting. The ideas look ever so much like a restatement of ideas from last year's plan but with new jargon." Surely he must be wrong, he thought. "These are experts, and the Director has every confidence in their work. Could it be that I am unfit for my office? It will never do for me to tell that I could not see anything worthwhile in the document."

"Haven't you anything to say about it?" asked one of the consultants as he went on working. "It is interesting—interesting, indeed!" answered the Associate Director, as he peered through his glasses. "What a ground-breaking plan!" "You'll report your observations to the Director?" the consultant asked. "Yes, I shall tell the Director that I am very impressed with your work," replied the Associate Director.

Several weeks later, the Director sent the legal counsel of the organization to see how the project was coming along and whether it would soon be ready. He fared just as the first: he looked and looked. "Isn't that an impressive piece of work?" asked the two consultants; and they displayed and explained the bold, new plan that was not there at all.

"I am an attorney. Surely I am neither incapable nor ineffective!" thought the counsel. "Yet it must be that I am not fit for my position. If that is the case, I must not let it be known." And so he praised the new plan, and expressed pleasure at its scope and far-reaching implications. "It is most innovative," he reported back to the Director.

Word spread, and soon all the people in the organization were talking of the visionary plan. The Director wished to see it herself while it was still in draft form. With her team of managers, including the two colleagues who had already reviewed the documents, she went to the office where the two consultants were working. The consultants turned on the computer and the best LCD projector money could buy and projected PowerPoint® highlights of the not-so-new plan.

"Isn't that splendid?" said the Associate Director. "Truly visionary," noted the attorney.

"Do you approve of the approach and direction?" the consultants asked the Director, as they pointed to the computer.

"What's this?" thought the Director. "I can make no sense of it at all! It appears to be nothing more than our old plan with new lingo. But my colleagues reached a very different conclusion. Am I not visionary? Am I not fit to be the Director of this great organization?" She thought for a moment and responded, "Oh, it is very interesting, indeed! Out-of-the box and state-of-the-art—just as you promised. I give it my highest approval."

The consultants printed out the documents, even made PDF versions, and submitted them with a final bill. The Director thanked the consultants appreciatively for their excellent work and its far-reaching contributions to the future of the organization.

*   *   *

A topic as intriguing, pervasive, and complex as leadership deserves attention. And from a walk down the bookstore aisle, there is plenty of evidence that the subject is receiving its just due. Leadership is the focus not only of satire and biography, but also of many new books and articles in business and professional areas. It is also the theme, though less obviously so, of the many publications that talk about the necessity of taking charge of one's own life and one's relationships, and of those that discuss strategies and skills to realize such aspirations.

The literature on leadership is vast and diverse. Some might say that it borders on being overwhelming. What Leaders Need to Know and Do began as a project to make some personal sense of the enormity of work on the subject. I wanted to develop a framework for organizing the extensive professional literature on leadership in a manner that would be helpful to me conceptually, and that would be useful as a guide for designing and evaluating leadership development courses and programs on which a number of us were working.[1] The result was the creation of the framework presented in this book as well as what has come to be called the Leadership Competencies Scorecard printed on pages 59–63 and offered on CD-ROM with this book. Both have been extremely useful for me personally. They have also been invaluable in leadership course and program development and evaluation at Rutgers. It is my hope that readers will find the ideas presented here equally helpful in their own personal and professional endeavors.

---

[1] These courses and programs were being developed for undergraduate and graduate students in organizational studies (Connaughton and Ruben 2004; Connaughton, Lawrence, and Ruben 2003) and also for executive and leadership development programs (http://www.odl.rutgers.edu/). The literature review also provided an important input to the development of the *Leadership Style Inventory (LSI): Becoming a Strategic Leader* (Ruben 2006).

The Quest for Excellence in Leadership

There was a time when the prevailing view of the exemplary leader was of a dominant, all-knowing individual who led his or her organization in a top-down, tough-minded, command-and-control fashion.

The leader needed to have all the answers, project self-confidence at all times, and be skilled at deflecting criticism or questioning, never yielding a position or point of view, particularly in public. Being anything less than fully prepared for a situation was being inept, and knowing less about a subject than those in subordinate positions was evidence of incompetence. Being reflective, wrong, or sorry were unmistakable signs of weaknesses.

Leadership: A Diverse Portfolio of Competencies

Some of the qualities we associate with the classical approach to leadership are admirable, and in various situations they may even be essential. In recent years, however, there is growing awareness that there is considerably more to excellence in leadership than was implied by the traditional view.

The challenges today's leaders face are daunting to say the least. With so many pressing needs, so many points of view, generally limited resources, and often very little time, how is a leader to successfully fulfill his or her responsibilities? Is it realistic to expect a leader to have all the answers and be more informed on all topics than those who report to him or her? Is the command-and-control, top-down model the most successful brand of leadership? Is it the most effective way to make good decisions, create commitment and buy-in, foster creative and innovative thinking, and make the most of the resources and talents of one's colleagues? Is it necessarily a sign of weakness if a leader says, "I'm not sure," "I don't understand," "I've changed my position," or "I apologize"? Or could it be a sign of strength? Good questions all, with no simple answers. Increasingly, we have come to recognize that there is no single prescription for leadership excellence, no one formula that ensures success across contexts and circumstances. To address the complex array of challenges they face, leaders need a broad array of knowledge and skills—a diverse portfolio of leadership competencies—and the ability to analyze situations and employ those competencies as needed.

What Leaders Need to Know and Do: A Leadership Competencies Scorecard is designed to describe and explain that portfolio. The pages ahead will introduce readers to a framework that surveys, summarizes, and synthesizes a broad cross section of the contemporary writings on leadership. The book organizes that literature into five broad competency areas, each of which is composed of a number of themes, and provides a Leadership Competencies Scorecard Inventory that allows readers to assess their leadership knowledge and skills in 35 critical competency areas. As is discussed later, the term competency was selected to convey the sense that both understanding and skill in implementation are vital for leadership excellence; knowledge of leadership concepts informs practice, and vice versa.

In addition, the Leadership Competencies Scorecard functions as a helpful tool for planning, developing, and implementing leadership development courses or programs, and readers will find an explanation of how the framework can be used in that way. The purpose of this book, then, is to provide a literature-based framework that summarizes current thinking on the knowledge and skill set needed to address the complex array of challenges that awaits contemporary leaders and those involved with leadership development.

chapter 1

What Leaders Need to Know

Leadership has become a popular topic of study in recent years, and it is the theme of countless academic, professional, and trade books and articles. The result is an expansive, diverse, and sometimes overwhelming assortment of theories, observations, assertions, insights, and advice.

For those trying to make sense of these writings, and, even more so, for those seeking practical, professional guidance on how to be an effective leader, this situation presents a substantial challenge.

Defining Leadership

Even a quick review of contemporary works on leadership reveals a wide variety of perspectives on the nature of leadership. The following are some writers' answers to the question "What is leadership?":

- **Advancing societal values (Gardner 1968).**

    "Leaders... serve as symbols of the moral unity of the society [and] articulate goals that lift people out of their petty preoccupations, carry them above the conflicts that tear a society apart, and unite them in pursuit of objects worthy of their best efforts."

- **"Attracting people and making things happen" (Maxwell 1999, ix).**

- **Balancing values (Barrett 1998).**

    Leaders are engaged in "finding a dynamic balance between the interest of the corporation, the interest of the workers, the interest of the local community, and the interest of society" (2–3).

    "The world is searching for a new type of... leadership—one that is able to operationalize win-win opportunities... in a... culture that supports social responsibility, environmental stewardship, and employee fulfillment" (2).

- **Closing the gap between what people know and what they do.**

    "We live in a world where knowledge transfer and information exchange are tremendously efficient, and where there are numerous organizations in the business of collecting and transferring best practices. So, there are fewer and smaller differences in what firms know than in their ability to act on that knowledge." (Leadership is about closing that gap.) (Pfeffer and Sutton 2000, 243).

- **Creating a vision and translating that vision into action (Useem 1998).**

    "Leaders manage the dream. All leaders have the capacity to create a compelling vision, one that takes people to a new place, and the ability to translate that vision into reality" (Bennis 1999, 26).

- **Building community (DePree 1999, 16).**

  Leaders are creators and sustainers of culture (Schein 1996).

- **Communication.**

  "Leadership is first and foremost a communication process, or set of processes. Every leadership behavior is enacted through communication" (Witherspoon 2004, 2).

- **Collaborating and encouraging the pursuit of mutually beneficial purposes (Hackman and Johnson 2000, 12).**

- **Creating images that engage.**

  "Leadership is an essentially social phenomenon: without followers there are no leaders. What leaders must do, therefore, is construct an imaginary communication that followers can feel part of. In this case the imagination of the followers is critical, because few will ever know their fellow community well enough really to know whether they have anything in common" (Grint 2000, 7; based on B. Anderson, *Imagined Communities: Reflections on the Origin and Spread of Nationalism* [London: Verso, 1991], 6).

- **Influencing individual or group behavior.**

  Leadership is "any attempt to influence the behavior of another individual or group" (Hersey 1984, 14).

  Leadership is the "art of influencing people by persuasion or example to follow a line of action" (DuBrin 2004, 3).

- **Influencing the community to face its problems (Heifetz 1994, 14; Heifetz and Linsky 2002).**

  "Leaders... challenge us to face problems for which there are no simple, painless solutions—problems that require us to learn new ways" (Heifetz 1994, 2).

Leadership is about adaptive work. "Adaptive work consists of the learning required to address conflicts in the values people hold, or to diminish the gap between the values people stand for and the reality they face" (22).

- **Managing change.**

  Leadership is encouraging "change in order to meet the needs or to reach the goals of a group (task force, business organization, social movement, state legislature, military unit, nation)" (Hackman and Johnson 2000, 11).

  Leadership is "preparing organizations for change and helping them cope as they struggle through it" (Kotter 2001).

- **Managing language.**

  "Leadership is a language game." Language is a tool of influence. "Leaders operate in uncertain, sometimes chaotic environments that are partly of their own creation; while leaders do not control events, they do influence how events are seen and understood" (Fairhurst and Sarr 1996, xi).

- **Motivating others to achieve goals.**

  Leaders demonstrate the "ability to inspire and stimulate others to achieve worthwhile goals" (DuBrin 2004, 3).

- **Solving problems.**

  Leadership in the public sector entails "solving problems in highly interconnected political and inter-organizational contexts in which authority is shared and power is fragmented." It also involves focusing attention and mobilizing "sustained action by multiple and diverse stakeholders to address issues usually defined in terms of desired outcomes or results" (Luke 1998, 5).

Copyright 2006 by Randy Glasbergen.
www.glasbergen.com

GLASBERGEN

"My team has created a very innovative solution,
but we're still looking for a problem to go with it."

- **Validating value and worth.**

   "Leadership is communicating people's worth and potential so clearly
   that they are inspired to see it in themselves" (Covey 2004, 98).

The variety of views on leadership does not end with basic defini-
tions. In the literature, one encounters a number of what are described
as important distinctions between contrasting ways of thinking about
leadership. Burns (1978) and others (Bass 1990b; Bass and Avolio
1990; Luke 1998), for example, differentiate between transactional
and transformational leadership. Transactional leadership is seen as
involving an exchange between the leader and follower (e.g., wages,
gifts, votes, prestige, etc.—it can be economic, political, or psychologi-
cal). The idea is that the leader provides items of value to followers
in exchange for their following the leader's wishes or contributing to
efforts to meet the leader's goals. Transformational leadership, on the
other hand, is described as a circumstance wherein leaders create a
shared sense of purpose, tapping existing motives or aspirations, mov-
ing away from narrow, personal interests to focus on communal and
shared interests—shared by both leaders and followers.

A number of authors also distinguish between what are often referred to as the trait, style, and contingency approaches to leadership. Trait theories focus on an individual's inherent capabilities, based "... on the assumption that the individual is more important than the situation" (Handy 1993, 97). Style theories focus on the critical role played by an individual's personal and leadership approach, and contingency theories emphasize the nature of the match between a leader's behavior, on the one hand, and the situation, on the other (96–115).

The distinction between leadership and management is also common in the literature (DuBrin 2004; Kotter 2001; Mintzberg 1973; Zaleznik 1992). From Kotter's (2001, 86) viewpoint, "Management is about coping with complexity. Leadership, by contrast, is about coping with change." Luke (1998) asserts that it is important to distinguish between the public and the private sectors to understand the nature of leadership. Not surprisingly, textbooks on leadership typically provide an overview and discussion of a number of these distinctions (Komives, Lucas, and McMahon 1998, 34–47; Northouse 2004, 15–122; Witherspoon 1997).

Creating a Leadership Scorecard

As intellectually provocative as is this array of perspectives on leadership, the richness and diversity are perhaps not very helpful to someone seeking an integrated understanding of leadership or guidelines for effective leadership practice.

This book addresses the problem by summarizing and synthesizing various views on leadership and providing an integrated, competency-based model of leadership that answers the fundamental question: What do leaders need to know and be able to do?

To answer that question, a cross section of approximately 100 books and articles on leadership was reviewed.[1]

[1] The review focused on academic texts and professional books and articles on leadership; it excluded biographies and academic research articles.

For each source, the goal was to identify what the author or authors describe as critical facets of leadership. In all, more than 400 unique facets of leadership were identified. Next, those were organized into 35 leadership themes based on the descriptions. Those, in turn, were grouped into five leadership competency areas. Collectively, the five competency areas and the 35 themes that make them up form the Leadership Competencies Scorecard presented in this book. The five competency areas are listed below and illustrated in Figure 1:

1.   Analytic competencies

2.   Personal competencies

3.   Communication competencies

4.   Organizational competencies

5.   Positional competencies

Figure 2 shows an overview of the areas of competency and their defining themes. The competencies, themes, sources, and facets of leadership are discussed in some detail in the following pages.

FIGURE 1—Leadership Competency Areas

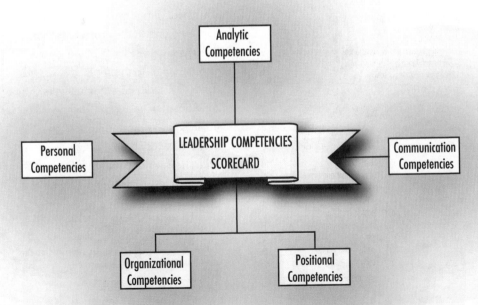

Following that discussion, a Leadership Competencies Scorecard
Inventory (LCSI) is provided for you to use in assessing your own leadership strengths and areas in need of improvement. As is explained in
more detail later, the LCSI can also be used as the basis for planning or
evaluating leadership development workshops, courses, or programs.

FIGURE 2—Leadership Themes in the Five Competency Areas

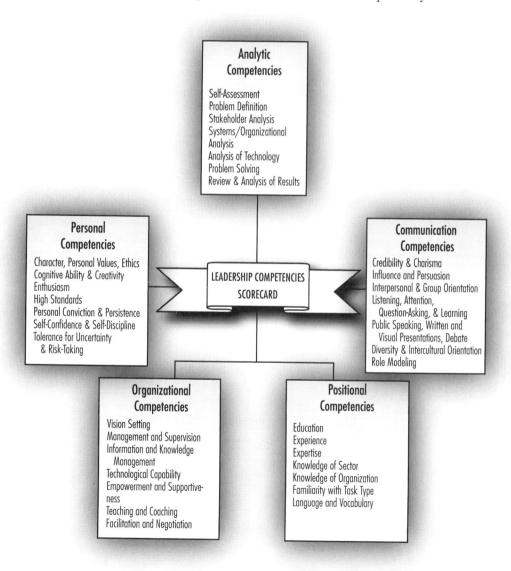

Analytic Competencies

It is perhaps not all that obvious, but analysis is one of the more important aspects of leadership. Analytic competencies refers to the knowledge and skills necessary for being self-aware, clarifying situations and problems, considering alternative leadership strategies, selecting effective strategies, solving problems, and evaluating outcomes.

In the terminology used on the Leadership Scorecard, this leadership competency area includes the following themes: *self-assessment; problem definition; stakeholder analysis; systems/organizational analysis; analysis of technology available to support leadership; problem solving;* and *review and analysis of results.* Each of these themes highlights a facet of leadership that is essential to success.

ANALYTIC COMPETENCIES

✓   Self-Assessment

✓   Problem Definition

✓   Stakeholder Analysis

✓   Systems/Organizational Analysis

✓   Analysis of Technology

✓   Problem Solving

✓   Review and Analysis of Results

Self-Assessment

Self-assessment refers to the need for leaders to understand themselves, know who they are, recognize their strengths and liabilities, realize their personal vulnerabilities, and acknowledge their motives, goals, and reactions. Many writers talk about such capabilities in terms of the need for self-knowledge and self-awareness (Benton 1998; Benfari 1999; Bennis and Nanus 1985; Goleman 1998; Komives, Lucas, and McMahon 1998, 108–34; Mintzberg 1990; Useem 1998, 266; Kouzes and Posner 1995, xxi).

Others describe this competency simply as knowing yourself (Maxwell 1999; Useem 1998, 266) and note the importance of using the knowledge you have of yourself to guide your leadership (Noyes 2001). Maxwell (1999, 47) talks about the need to "listen to your gut." In addition to its other virtues, self-awareness enhances one's capacity for self-development (Kouzes and Posner 1995, 336–40) and makes possible recruiting colleagues who have strengths in areas where a leader has weaknesses (Maxwell 1999, 56).

Problem Definition

In general terms, problem definition refers to the need for leaders to be adept at determining the essence of a problem or challenge. There are always many ways to think about a problem, and in any situation one may be confronted with as many different views as there are involved parties. A critical capability of a leader is to see, understand, and sort through multiple perspectives (Bolman & Deal, 1997; Luke 1998, 226–27) and, through careful reasoning and analysis, to identify the key issues (Sorcher and Brant 2002). A fundamental aspect of problem solving is what Tichy describes as maintaining a perspective that is realistic and accurate: "See reality—size up the current situation as it really is, not as it used to be or as [one] would like it to be" (1997, 28).

Effective problem definition involves deciding how to frame and reframe problems (Luke 1998, 63). In defining a leadership problem, it is vital to distinguish between tasks that are structured and straight-forward and those that are unstructured, complex, and open (Handy 1993, 110). Closely related is the notion that leaders must be able to distinguish between what Heifetz (1994) terms "technical" problems and others he labels "adaptive" problems. Technical problems are those one can address by applying current know-how or routines. In contrast, adaptive problems involve "disparity between values and circumstances" [at hand] and these kinds of situations demand innovation, change and learning (35).

In addition, problem definition requires a leader to be skilled at discerning the specific needs that must be addressed in a given situation. This means the person has to be able to determine when a problem has primarily to do with completion of a task, when it involves interpersonal and group maintenance issues, when the fundamental problem has to do with the agendas of particular individuals (Adair 1983), and when cultural issues are central (Hofstede 1993; Schein 1992).

Stakeholder Analysis

Stakeholders are individuals, groups, organizations, or communities that may influence, or be influenced by, a leader's decisions or actions (Ruben 2005b). Stakeholder analysis relates to the necessity for leaders to be adept at identifying and taking account of the relevant constituencies in any situation, as well as being aware of the "ripple effect" that often occurs between and among those groups (Luke 1998, 70–72).

Speaking in particular of the public sector, Luke points to the indispensability of carefully assessing stakeholders, and those he terms "knowledgeholders," in order to become aware of and appropriately address the needs and concerns of each group with a vested interest in the process or outcomes, and also to take full advantage of those with relevant knowledge (1998, 70–72). He also emphasizes the importance of considering the "multiplicity of stakeholders involved with each public problem" (13). The consideration of stakeholders and knowledgeholders should look at appropriate ways of engaging and communicating with each constituency (Reeves 2002a, 153–249; Ruben 2004, 31–63; 2005b, 33–38).

Systems/Organizational Analysis

Systems and organizational thinking refers to the ability to grasp the big picture—to understand parts, wholes, and connections (Bolman and Deal 1997; Komives, Lucas, and McMahon 1998, 51–53). Handy describes this capacity as the "helicopter factor—the ability to rise above the particulars of a situation and perceive it in its relations to the overall environment" (Handy 1993, 99).

As described by various authors, it consists of "tuning into the environment: sensing needs and opportunities" (Kanter 2001, 258–61); seeing the bigger picture (DuBrin 2004, 53; Maxwell 1999, 47); broadly understanding organizational structures and dynamics (Komives, Lucas, and McMahon 1998, 198–225; Senge 1990; Wheatley 1999); understanding frameworks and framing (Bolman and Deal 1997); and understanding relevant cultural issues (Hofstede 1993).

Heifetz nicely captures the importance of systems thinking for leadership with the following example: "When a car fails to start in the morning, a mechanic rarely locates the problem in the key switch itself, but several feet away in the battery, starter, an electrical connection, or the alternator" (1994, 3).

Systems thinking is essential to the conceptualizations of problems and situations and to the mental models that leaders form (Luke 1998). Those mental models "are networks of familiar facts, ideas, and concepts with specific yet simplified cause-and-effect relationships" (12).

"To understand complex, intertwined problems, individuals develop and carry a 'mental model,' or internalized picture, of what a problem is, what is causing it, and how to solve it" (12).

From an operational perspective, systems analysis should include consideration of the power position of a leader in the total organization, the organizational norms, the structure and technology of the organization, the variety of tasks, and the number and variety of subordinates (Handy 1993, 112).

Analysis of Technology to Support Leadership

Twenty, perhaps even 10, years ago, one might not find much discussion of the role of technology in a forum on what leaders need to know. But things have changed. Increasingly, communication and information technologies play a vital role in organizing and organization, and for leaders, understanding the potential uses of technology in support of their efforts is critical. One of the more essential leadership competen-

cies in this regard is the capacity to assess geographic considerations within a group or organization and to select appropriate technology (Luke 1998, 9).

Today's leaders need an understanding of the appropriate uses of "E-Culture": "The World Wide Web is both the stimulus for a new organizational culture (making it necessary) and a facilitator of that same culture (making it possible)" (Kanter 2001, 6).

Leaders benefit greatly from a knowledge of the appropriate uses of virtual teams (Majchrzak et al. 2004) and need to be familiar with available communication and information technologies, and the attributes and potential liabilities of each, as they may be used in organizational and leadership endeavors (Connaughton and Ruben 2004; Connaughton and Daly 2003; 2004).

Problem Solving

Problem solving is a competency area of considerable focus in the literature on leadership. Competencies in this area include planning, discovering root causes of problems, reviewing past situations, learning how others think, evaluating options, identifying priorities, and selecting an appropriate action or response (DuBrin 2004; Kouzes and Posner 1995, 173–74; Maxwell 1999; Reeves 2002a, 99–111; Tichy 1997, 32; Tromp and Ruben 2004). Also relevant is the capacity to evaluate potential gains and losses associated with particular decisions (DuBrin 2004; Kouzes and Posner 1995, 172–73); to conduct a SWOT analysis to clarify strengths, weaknesses, opportunities, and threats (DuBrin 2004, 407–9); and to determine the best time to act (Goodwin 1999, 34; Kouzes and Posner 1996, 101–2).

In discussing problem solving, some writers talk about the importance of what they call context analysis (Bennis 1989, 13–37; Fairhurst and Sarr 1996, 82). As described, context analysis includes determining who is involved, what the various parties' interests are, what the possibilities for action are, what the leader's limitations are, where gaps in understanding exist, when the leader can best intervene, why people are responding as they are, why a new frame or approach is needed, and how a new frame can be established (Fairhurst and Sarr 1996, 82).

Luke (1998) identifies several factors that complicate problem solving for leaders in the public sector: problems cross traditional boundaries, and therefore require cross-boundary thinking; problems are socially constructed, and generally there is no natural consensus on problem definition; and often there are neither optimal solutions nor quick fixes or easy remedies. From Luke's perspective, much of the uniqueness in the public organizations results from the fact that "solving problems [in the public sector occurs] in highly interconnected political and inter-organizational contexts in which authority is shared and power is fragmented" (5).

Practically speaking, selecting an appropriate decision-making style and strategy is one of the more critical facets of problem solving (DuBrin 2004; Fiedler 1967; Hersey and Blanchard 1979; Vroom and Yetton 1973). Based on the situation at hand, a leader needs to determine whether to:

- Solve the problem or make the decision oneself, using information one has.

- Obtain the necessary information from subordinates, and then decide on the solution oneself.

- Share the problem with relevant subordinates individually, getting their ideas and suggestions, and then make the decision oneself.

- Share the problem with subordinates in a group, and then make the decision oneself.

- Share the problem with subordinates as a group, and then make the decision together. (Vroom and Yetton 1973)

In a similar vein, DuBrin (2004, 148–49) lists the following problem-solving options:

- Deciding oneself
- Consulting (individuals)
- Consulting (the group)
- Facilitating
- Delegating

"I would like you to be more self-reliant, show more initiative, and take greater personal responsibility — but check with me first!"

Finally, in selecting options it is important to distinguish between circumstances in which one has authority to "make things happen" from other situations in which leadership must rely on informal and indirect influence strategies (Heifetz 1994, 35).

Review and Analysis of Results

The ability to analyze and learn from history is an important capability for leaders in a wide variety of settings. DePree (1993, 30) talks about this in terms of analyzing and reviewing results in order to compare one's plans with outcomes, assess the impact of actions on key publics, and more specifically, evaluate the results of appointments and promotions.

In practical terms, the review and analysis of results assumes that a leader is committed to seeking, soliciting, and accepting feedback and critique on his or her own and/or the organization's performance (Maxwell 1999, 129). It also assumes that he or she has qualitative and quantitative information available relative to performance, and this in turn implies that leaders should promote the creation and implementation of "outcome-based information and feedback systems" (Kaplan and Norton 1996; 2001; Luke 1998, 139; Ruben 2004; 2005; Tromp and Ruben 2004). Without systematic methods for gathering data on outcomes and achievements within the organization, any effort to review and analyze results is of limited value, at best.

Personal Competencies

Personal competencies are among the most familiar in classic discussions of leadership, and they are frequent topics in writings on leadership. Competencies that fall in this category include character, values, and ethics; cognitive ability and creativity; enthusiasm; high standards; personal conviction and persistence; self-confidence and self-discipline; and tolerance for uncertainty and risk taking.

Character, Personal Values, and Ethics

Many authorities consider the leader's character, personal values, and ethical standards to be essential to his or her ability to lead. For each of these, knowledge and the ability to put that understanding into practice, are essential. Maxwell describes character as a choice; a leader's behavior expresses a personal set of values and beliefs (DePree 1993, 3). "We have no

PERSONAL COMPETENCIES

✓ Character, Personal Values, and Ethics

✓ Cognitive Ability and Creativity

✓ Enthusiasm

✓ High Standards

✓ Personal Conviction and Persistence

✓ Self-Confidence and Self-Discipline

✓ Tolerance for Uncertainty and Risk Taking

control over a lot of things in life.... [such as family, location of birth, upbringing, talents, or IQ]. But we do choose our character.... we create it every time we make choices" (Maxwell 1999, 5). Furthermore, Maxwell writes, "Followers do not trust leaders whose character they know to be flawed, and they will not continue to follow them" (5).

Ethical conduct is also essential (Komives, Lucas, and McMahon 1998; Luke 1998, 236–39; Northouse 2004, 301–27). "Leadership is a matter of how to be, not how to do" (Hasselbein 1999, vii). According to Hackman and Johnson, leaders must learn to cope successfully with a variety of ethical dilemmas relating to honesty, responsibility, power, and loyalty (2000, x).

In discussing particular dimensions of character and specific personal values and ethical standards that are essential for leaders, many authors comment on the importance of honesty and integrity (Drucker 1999, 5; Sorcher and Brant 2002; Handy 1993, 99; Kirkpatrick and Locke 1991; Komives, Lucas, and McMahon 1998, 247–73). Luke talks about the importance of what he terms "exemplary personal integrity" (1998, 228–36), and DePree (1993) believes integrity precedes all else. Pfeffer and Sutton describe this issue in terms of "conducting business with uncompromising integrity" (2000, 75).

Trustworthiness is another topic of considerable discussion in the contemporary literature (Bennis and Nanus 1985; DePree 1993, 159; DuBrin 2004, 33). Some writers explain that "fear and distrust

"I've tried to be passionate about my career,
but my career just wants to be good friends."

undermine organizational performance" (Pfeffer and Sutton 2000, 109), and note that "driving fear out starts at the top—just as paranoia does" (130).

The value of humility is also mentioned as an important leadership capability (Badaracco 2001; Collins 2001; DuBrin 2004, 33; McGarvey 2004). According to Collins, leaders of organizations that move from "good to great" promote the organization, not themselves (2001, 21–22). Such leaders are often "self-effacing, quiet, reserved, even shy" (14).

Other leader characteristics mentioned in the literature include believing in other people (Bennis 1989, 202; Kouzes and Posner 1996, 106–7); being oneself (Kelleher 1999, 43); courage (Handy 1993, 99; DuBrin 2004, 43; Useem 1998); equity (DePree 1993, 11; Reeves 2002b, [2002a or 2002b] 16–18); generosity with one's time, talent, money, or possessions (Maxwell 1999; McGarvey 2004); responsibility and dependability (Stogdill 1948); and a sense of humor (DuBrin 2004, 33). Prince (1998) thinks moral development is essential for competent leadership, and Hewertson (2002), McGarvey (2004), and Tichy (1997) underscore the importance of a values orientation.

The desires to serve and to exercise social and civic responsibility
are seen by many as critical values for leadership (Komives, Lucas, and
McMahon 1998, 15). What Greenleaf (1977, 2002) terms "servant
leadership"—which refers to a commitment to serve and to help others—is an important leadership value about which a good deal has
been written (Spears and Lawrence 2002; Bennis 2002; Covey 2002;
DePree 2002). Heifetz asserts that leaders should be dedicated to
socially responsible outcomes, which he defines as "producing socially
useful outcomes by setting goals that meet the needs of both the leader
and followers" (1994, 20). Having moral purpose and values (Fullan
2001; DuBrin 2004; Reeves, 2002b) and demonstrating concern for
others (Luke 1998, 227–28) are also described as important for leaders. DuBrin (2004) focuses specifically on the importance of moral
leadership and being principled in ethics, which he sees as consisting
of five ethical leadership behaviors: (1) being honest and trustworthy
and having integrity in dealing with others; (2) paying attention to all
stakeholders; (3) building community; (4) respecting the individual; and
(5) accomplishing silent victories through modesty and restraint.

A somewhat different view is expressed by Kellerman (2004). He
does not see leadership as a moral concept at all, noting that one can
learn as much about leadership from "bad" examples as good ones.
Leaders, Kellerman says, are like the rest of us—not all moral, flawless,
and truthful in all situations, in all ways.

Cognitive Ability and Creativity

Whether termed intelligence or cognitive ability, a person's general
intellectual capacity has traditionally been considered when describing effective leadership (Stogdill 1948). In recent years, various writers
continue to assert the view that cognitive ability is important, but they
do so in more inclusive terms (Handy 1993; Kirkpatrick and Locke
1991). Handy, for example, says leaders should be of "above average but
not a genius level" (1993, 98). And, speaking somewhat more generally, Bennis (1989, 202) points to the importance of leaders having a
broadly based education.

A number of authors focus on the need for leaders to develop their creativity, originality, and imagination (Bennis 1989, 202; Du-Brin 2004, 15, 332–36; Handy 1993, 99; and Kirkpatrick and Locke 1991). They see creativity as the key to innovation and to "stimulating breakthrough ideas," through what Kanter calls "kaleidoscope thinking" (2001, 261–64).

Enthusiasm

It might seem obvious to note that leaders should be enthusiastic (DuBrin 2004, 33; Bennis 1989, 202; Handy 1993, 99). Enthusiasm is a great advantage when it comes to creating a following for one's ideas, projects, or goals. In Luke's (1998, 223–24) terms, a passion toward outcomes is a great asset for a leader.

Speaking a bit more generally, Maxwell reminds us that "attitude is a choice.... your attitude determines your actions" (1999, 91). Benton (1998, 117–32) makes a similar point when he talks about the impor-

"This light warns you that your battery may be critically low. And *this* light warns you that your conversation may be critically dull."

tance of what he terms "attitude management." Both writers, each in their own way, emphasize the extent to which a leader can exercise conscious choice over the level of energy, enthusiasm, and passion he or she brings to his or her work, and they remind us that such choices often have significant consequences for the effectiveness of the leader.

High Standards

Valuing, establishing, maintaining, and displaying high standards for oneself and others is imperative for leaders, according to a number of writers (Bennis 1989, 202; Drucker 1999, 4–5; Handy 1993, 119; Kouzes and Posner 1995; Useem 1998, 266). Indeed, Reeves (2002b, 5) goes so far as to characterize the establishment and maintenance of standards as one of the essential keys to leadership.

Personal Conviction and Persistence

Across a wide range of people and situations, personal conviction and commitment are essential facets of successful leadership (Kouzes and Posner 1995, 139). Stephen Gregg, chairman and CEO of Ethix Corp., is emphatic on this point: "People do not follow uncommitted leaders. Commitment can be displayed in a full range of matters to include the work hours you choose to maintain, how you work to improve your abilities, or what you do for your fellow workers at personal sacrifice" (Maxwell 1999, 15).

A number of writers also talk specifically about the value of persistence or perseverance—a quality described variously as adhering to a sense of purpose over time (Bennis 1982; Heifetz 1994, 275–79; Kanter 2001, 274–79; Stogdill 1948; Kirkpatrick and Locke 1991), being tenacious, and remaining steadfast in one's pursuits (Useem 1998, 266).

Self-Confidence and Self-Discipline

Good leadership requires discipline (Kouzes and Posner 1995, 76–77). Maxwell recommends that leaders make a disciplined lifestyle a per-

© 1998 Randy Glasbergen.

GLASBERGEN

**"The last thing I remember, I was sitting in a
staff meeting. Apparently, I died from boredom."**

sonal goal (Maxwell 1999, 128) and suggests that they aim to achieve
one specific goal every day (93). In a similar vein, DuBrin (2004, 19)
advocates the need for a strong work ethic. Self-discipline can also
be essential in terms of maintaining control of one's emotions and
behavior—a critical element of what Goleman (1998) and others have
termed emotional intelligence.

Authors describe self-assurance and self-confidence as fundamental
for successful leadership in a variety of circumstances (Bennis, 1985;
DuBrin 2004, 33; Handy 1993, 99, 119; Kirkpatrick and Locke 1991;
Noyes 2001).

Tolerance for Uncertainty and Risk Taking

The literature devotes considerable attention to the theme of tolerance
for uncertainty, chaos, and risk taking; tolerance for all three is widely
acknowledged as essential to effective leadership in today's environment (Bennis 1989, 143–45; DuBrin 2004, 33; Handy 1993, 109, 119;
Heifetz and Linsky 2002, 9–48; Kanter 2001, 6, 255–84; Komives,

Lucas, and McMahon 1998, 48–49; Kouzes and Posner 1995, 51; Tichy 1997, 20; Wheatley 1999). There's no doubt leaders in all sectors are confronted by complexity and fast-paced change, and in the face of uncertainty and rapid change, composure, flexibility, adaptability, entrepreneurial behavior, and) crisis management capabilities are great virtues (Crutcher 2004; DuBrin 2004, 15; Handy 1993, 109; DuBrin 2004, 43, 156–58; Fullan 2001; Kirkpatrick and Locke 1991).

Change leadership and effectiveness as a change agent are also perceived to be crucial capabilities for leaders (Conger and Benjamin 1999; Conger, Spreitzer, and Lawler 1999; Kanter 2001, 6, 229–53; Kouzes and Posner 1995, 51; Komives, Lucas, and McMahon 1998, 7–8; Pfeffer and Sutton 2000; Reeves 2002a, 21–47). Building a broad organizational commitment to change is an important facet of change management, especially in situations where one's authority alone is insufficient to bring about the intended action (Senge 1996).

chapter 5

Communication Competencies

Discussions of leadership often center on communication, and a number of writers see communication as the most fundamental of the leadership competencies (Witherspoon 2004, 2; Bennis and Nanus, 1985).

Witherspoon, for example, asserts that "leadership is first and foremost a communication process" (2004, 2). And, "Every leadership behavior is enacted through communication" (2). Goodwin is another who emphasizes these competencies, describing language as one of the leader's most powerful tools (1999, 35).

The major themes to be considered within the broader category of leadership communication are *credibility and charisma; influence and persuasion; interpersonal and group orientation;*

COMMUNICATION COMPETENCIES

✓ Credibility and Charisma

✓ Influence and Persuasion

✓ Interpersonal and Group Orientation

✓ Listening, Attention, Question-Asking, and Learning

✓ Public Speaking, Written and Visual Presentation, and Debate

✓ Diversity and Intercultural Orientation

✓ Role Modeling

listening, attention, question-asking, and learning; public speaking, written and visual presentation, and debate; diversity and intercultural orientation; and role modeling.

Credibility and Charisma

Both understanding and skill are important to leader credibility and charisma. Credibility is often described as the ability to influence (Hackman and Johnson 2000, 162; Kirkpatrick and Locke 1991; Kouzes and Posner 1995). What factors lead one to be regarded as credible? Competence, trustworthiness, and dynamism, say Brumbeck and Howell (1976).

Often mentioned as a desirable trait of leaders, charisma is none-theless one of those terms that has a very imprecise meaning. Some describe charismatic leaders as envisioning, energizing, and enabling (Nadler and Tishman 1990). In other discussions, charisma seems to imply a spiritual or magical quality. Thinking about charisma from a communication perspective, however, adds clarity and precision, and the result is that the concept becomes much more useful for leaders. Rather than viewing it as an inherent, spiritual, or mystical attribute of the person, from a communication point of view we can see charisma as a characteristic of the *relationship* between the leader and other people (DuBrin 2004, 65–79). Following this line of reasoning, Maxwell, quoting Dan Reiling, vice president of leadership development at INJOY, offers some specific and practical advice for how to be regarded as a charismatic leader: "Be more concerned about making others feel good about themselves than you are making them feel good about you" (Maxwell 1999, 8).

Closely related to the concepts of credibility and charisma is admiration. Kouzes and Posner think being admired is an important leadership dimension, and characterize admired leaders as those who are regarded as honest, forward-looking, inspiring, competent, fair-minded, supportive, and broad-minded (1995, 21).

Influence and Persuasion

Influence and persuasion are among the most basic competencies associated with leadership communication (Tichy 1997, 36–37; Useem 1998, 266). Essentially, they involve motivating, guiding, directing, building coalitions and consensus, and/or gaining the commitment of others, often in order to bring about change (Conger and Benjamin 1999, 251; Goodwin 1999; Komives, Lucas, and McMahon 1998, 227–45; Maxwell 1999; Reeves 2002a, 21–47).

Often people are influential, at least in part, because they have positional power—they occupy roles or jobs that enable them to more easily sway others (Handy 1993, 124–31; DuBrin 2004, 194). Closely related to positional influence is the idea of authority. Heifetz describes authority as "conferred power to perform a service" (1994, 57). From the perspective of leadership communication, being in a position of authority can be quite beneficial. Authority (1) provides a holding environment for containing stresses; (2) commands and directs attention; (3) provides access to information; (4) ensures control over the flow of information; (5) provides power to frame issues; (6) allows one to orchestrate conflict; and (7) gives one the ability to choose the decision-making process (103–4).

Yet most circumstances afford opportunities for a person to influence others, even if he or she does not occupy a particular position or role (DuBrin 2004, 194). Therefore leaders should strive to become adept at being effective in situations where they do not have positional

© 1999 Randy Glasbergen.
www.glasbergen.com

GLASBERGEN

**"Let's form a committee to create a task force
to develop a team to determine the fastest
way to deal with the problem."**

power, as well as those where they do. In such situations, personal communication skills become especially critical. It is useful to recognize
that leading *without* authority also has advantages in terms of influence, according to Heifetz (1994, 188). In such cases one can more
easily deviate from the norms of authoritative decision making (e.g.,
one can ask questions that disturb, with no obligation to keep things
running smoothly). Those not in positions of authority are also not
required—as are formal leaders—to contend with the expectations
of multiple constituencies. One can have an issue focus, and one can
choose to identify more closely with the experiences of some—but not
necessarily all—of the stakeholders in the situation (188).

Operationally, Yukl and Tracey (1992, 525–35) list a number of options for influencing others, including physical power, resource power
(possession of valued resources), position power, role-based power
(control of information, right of access, right to organize), expert power,
acknowledged expertise, and personal power (personality, popularity,
appeal) (Summary provided by DuBrin 2004, 247–50). Kipnis et al.

(1984) provide a somewhat different list of strategies of influence: reason, friendliness, coalition building, bargaining, assertiveness, and appeals to a higher authority or the imposition of sanctions.

Another facet of persuasion and influence is impression management, which essentially involves efforts to influence the perceptions others have of a person—what Benton (1998, 133–56) calls "perception management." The idea of impression management is based on a 1959 work by Erving Goffman, *The Presentation of Self in Everyday Life* (Hackman and Johnson 2000, 24–25). As Goffman explained, leaders engage in the management of impressions to secure their leadership positions and to achieve their leadership goals. The same idea is used in military leadership, where impression management is talked about in terms of mask of command (Keegan 1987). See discussion in Hackman and Johnson (2000, 25).

The use of language and symbol plays a critical role in influence and persuasion. Language is used to create the image of reality for others through the manner in which messages are created, organized, and slanted—what is often described as framing (Bolman and Deal 1997; Fairhurst and Sarr 1996). Competent leaders are adept at using language to "mobilize action" and to find ways to frame, or reframe, situations so as to overcome obstacles (Pfeffer and Sutton 2000, 65–66). In addition to managing language, effective leaders use other symbols, artifacts, and rituals to influence the attitudes and behavior of others to reach their goals (Hackman and Johnson 2000, 27; Kouzes and Posner 1995, 228–29).

It's difficult to talk about persuasion and influence, as they relate to leadership, without talking about "politics." There's no doubt that political strategy, sensitivity, and savvy (DuBrin 2004, 15), or what Morrison (1992) terms "organizational savvy," can be extremely important for leaders.

At a general level, many authors talk about the importance of having a strategic approach to influence. DuBrin (2004, 213–15), for example, lists the following leadership strategies for political and power-gaining strategies: developing power contacts; controlling vital information; controlling lines of communication; bringing in outside experts; making a quick showing (produce dramatic results); and remembering that everyone expects to be paid back. Some additional communication strategies to enhance influence include these: leading with questions, not answers; engaging in dialogue and debate, not coercion; conducting (post-event) autopsies without blame; and building "red flag" mechanisms (early warning/information systems) (Collins 2001, 74–78).

In discussing the requirements of successful public leadership, Luke lists the following strategies as essential to influence (1998, 147):

- **Building commitment and political support**
  Multiple champions
  Support from those in power
  Constituent support
  Resources

- **Institutionalizing cooperative behavior**
  Action vehicles
  Self-organization groups
  Outcomes-based information system

- **Becoming a networking facilitator**
  Maintain focus on desired outcomes
  Develop and nurture relationships and trust
  Seek small wins
  Maintain commitment to learning
  Spiral back to earlier tasks to build on commitment

Strong relationships are essential to leadership effectiveness in so many respects. DuBrin suggests leaders do the following to develop relationships: display loyalty; manage impressions; ask those who have been satisfied with your work to offer endorsements to your supervisor; be courteous, pleasant, and positive; ask for advice; send thank-you notes to large numbers of people; and flatter and compliment others on their accomplishments (2004, 215–18). Leaders can use such strategies for purely altruistic reasons—to build and enhance relations with others—or in a more strategic manner to enhance influence and persuasion.

Copyright 2001 by Randy Glasbergen.
www.glasbergen.com

GLASBERGEN

"My team is having trouble thinking outside the box. We can't agree on the size of the box, what materials the box should be constructed from, a reasonable budget for the box, or our first choice of box vendors."

Various writers provide a valuable cautionary note: leadership influence is created and maintained not only by what one does, but also by what one is careful not to do. Essentially, the advice is to avoid political blunders (DuBrin 2004, 218–19). In particular, avoid criticizing a supervisor in a public forum; avoid bypassing one's supervisor; avoid declining an offer from top management (e.g., a promotion or special assignment) more than once; and avoid being tactless. This last bit of advice seems to imply that there are times when someone who can discern the difference between tactful and tactless behavior chooses to be purposefully tactless. We may question how often that circumstance actually occurs, but the advice is still useful if only to remind us of the importance of tact in persuasive communication.

Interpersonal and Group Orientation

Competency in one-to-one and group communication is a necessity for all leaders (Conger and Benjamin 1999, 250; Kouzes and Posner 1995, 142; Fullan 2001; Goleman 1998; Maxwell 1999; Noyes 2001;

Roser, Johnsrud, and Heck 2003). Simply stated, interpersonal and group orientation refers to the way one interacts with others (Komives, Lucas, and McMahon 1998, 165–74; Maxwell 1999).

These competencies serve a number of vital purposes, among them encouraging the expression of differing opinions and criticism (DePree 1993, 106); openly and authentically sharing oneself and one's points of view (141); working with followers to establish mutual purposes (Hackman and Johnson 2000); creating coalitions by enlisting backers and supporters (Kanter 2001, 267–72; Maxwell 1999, 11; McGarvey 2004); and dealing constructively with divisive colleagues (Reeves 2002b, 59, 71–72).

A great many specific facets of interpersonal and group communication are noted as important by writers on leadership. These include assertiveness (DuBrin 2004, 33); team building (Kanter 2001, 272–74); collaboration, cooperation, and being a team player (Crutcher 2004; Kouzes and Posner 1995, 151–57); earning respect (Drucker 1999, 6); inclusiveness; building trust (Goodwin 1999, 35; Handy 1993, 109; Kouzes and Posner 1995, 163–67); social skill and relationship building (Komives, Lucas, and McMahon 1998, 20–22, 68–102); nonverbal awareness (DuBrin 2004, 373–74; Goleman 1998; Maxwell 1999, 14); perspective taking (seeing another's perspective) empathy (Goleman 1998; Hackman and Johnson 2000, 182–83; McGarvey 2004); and conflict management (DuBrin 2004, 387–92).

Listening, Attention, Question-Asking, and Learning

Particularly in recent years, more and more leaders are recognizing the importance of devoting at least as much energy to gathering information as to sharing it. Of the competences that are essential to this goal, none is more basic than listening. Maxwell (1999) offers some practical advice to leaders: spend time listening. Arrange your time so that you dedicate time to listening to your followers, customers, competitors, and mentors. "Listen between the lines," Maxwell advises (79–80).

Listening is also the foundation for active learning (Crutcher 2004; Komives, Lucas, and McMahon 1998, 18–20; Kouzes and Posner 1995, 146–47, 168–69; Luke 1998, 95–96, 137–38; Reeves 2002b, 75–78).

As Tichy notes, "leaders [need to be] avid learners. They draw from their pasts and reflect on their experiences to develop lessons for the future" (1997, 23).

Maxwell comments: "To keep leading, keep learning" (1999, 141). He argues that "ironically, lack of teachability is often rooted in achievement" (144). To learn, it is important to "overcome your success" and "trade in your pride" (145). Speaking to leaders, Maxwell recommends "learning something new—today, each day" (147). Both listening and learning are greatly enhanced by skillful question-asking (Fine, 2005; Fontana, 1990; Hargie, Saunders & Dickson,1994; Maggio, 2005; Patterson & others, 2002; Young, 1999).

Public Speaking, Written and Visual Presentation, and Debate

Public speaking, presentation skills (verbal and visual), and debate are fundamental communication competencies for any leader. As Gilbert Amelio, president and CEO of National Semiconductor, said, "If a leader can't get a message across clearly and motivate others to act on it, then having a message doesn't even matter" (Maxwell 1999, 23). Leaders must be spokespersons and effective public speakers (DuBrin 2004, 14, 364–73; Hackman and Johnson 2000; Sorcher and Brant 2002).

Skillful and coherent presentations of one's ideas in written and visual channels are essential requirements for leadership (Fairhurst and Sarr 1996; Kouzes and Posner 1995; Connaughton and Ruben 2004). Through presentations, leaders increase visibility and awareness of problems and areas that need to be addressed and improved (Luke 1998, 95) and in the process shape others' perceptions of their leadership ability.

"Leaders [must] make full use of the power of language to communicate.... [They] use metaphors and figures of speech; they give examples, tell stories, and relate anecdotes; they draw word pictures; and they offer quotations and recite slogans" (Kouzes and Posner 1995, 134). At the most basic level, presentational competencies include basics such as spelling, grammar, and style, as well as clarity, organization, and audience appropriateness (Connaughton and Ruben 2004;

Ruben and Stewart, 2005). At a more general level, practical suggestions include these: explain yourself clearly (Useem 1998, 266); keep
messages simple and avoid the "mystique of complexity" (Pfeffer and
Sutton 2000, 51–54); and "simplify your message, see the person, show
the truth, seek a response" (Maxwell 1999, 26–27).

Debate, in the nontechnical sense of the term, refers to one's ability
to discuss issues in an effective manner and to promote particular points
of view. Competence in this facet of communication requires one to be
adept at listening to and understanding the various perspectives at play
in any situation. One must also be effective in persuasively articulating
a position while taking account of these differing viewpoints.

Diversity and Intercultural Orientation

Managing diversity has become a necessity for leadership (Hackman
and Johnson 2000, x), and sensitivity to issues of diversity is predicted
to gain importance in the future (Conger and Benjamin 1999).

Prentice (2004) explains the challenge simply: people are complex,
and people are different. Leaders, therefore, need to develop the knowledge and skills required to appreciate and work effectively with a diverse
array of colleagues. DePree notes that it is "impossible for a modern-day
organization to reach its potential—until through delegation a leader
brings to bear the diverse gifts of many individuals" (1993, 156–57).
To be successful in these ways, leaders need cultural, intercultural, and
international sensitivity (DuBrin 2004, 429–52; Hofstede 1993) and
the ability to overcome cross-cultural barriers (DuBrin 2004, 379–85).
Of parallel importance is a sensitivity to gender- and age-related issues
and lifestyle differences (Morrison 1992).

Role Modeling

Essentially, role modeling consists of translating one's vision (talk)
into action (Tichy 1997, 23). Kouzes and Posner (1995) describe this
as modeling the way.

As DePree notes, "The organization expects the leader to define and express both in writing and, especially, through behavior, the beliefs and values of the institution" (1993, 26). No doubt this is one of the more important leadership competencies, because if leaders fail to "walk the talk" or "practice what they preach or teach," it is doubtful that their verbalized vision or values will be taken seriously by colleagues. "Acting as a model for followers, a leader exemplifies higher purpose" (Luke 1998, 26).

One of the more important characteristics of role modeling is its focus on behavior. As Pfeffer and Sutton (2000) assert: talking is not the equivalent of doing. "One of the main barriers to turning knowledge into action is the tendency to treat talking about something as equivalent to actually doing something about it. Talking about what should be done, writing plans about what the organization should do, and collecting and analyzing data to help decide what actions to take are important activities and they can guide and motivate action. Indeed, rhetoric is frequently an essential first step toward taking action. But just talking about what needs to be done isn't enough. Something has to get done, and someone has to do it" (29). Translating talk into action is, thus, one of the most critical leadership competencies.

Practically speaking, role modeling is about being, and being seen as, competent; showing up every day; maintaining a commitment to continual improvement and follow-through; accomplishing more than is expected (Maxwell 1999, 33–34); and demonstrating the value of shared leadership (Pearce and Conger 2003). Perhaps most fundamentally, it is also about discovering and emphasizing core values in one's behavior (Collins and Porras 1997). "The legacy you leave is the life you live" (Kouzes and Posner 1996, 106–7).

chapter 6

Organizational Competencies

Many authors make clear that organizational knowledge and skill have an important place in the portfolio of competencies required for successful leadership. Critical themes in this area include vision setting; management and supervision; information and knowledge management; technological capability; empowerment and supportiveness; teaching and coaching; and facilitation and negotiation.

Vision Setting

Given the importance of a common, compelling, and inspiring vision, authors generally regard clearly articulating where a group or organization is headed as basic to good leadership. Vision defines the target, motivates the leader and others, and gives people "hope" (Maxwell 1999, 11). Adept leaders understand the importance of shared aspirations and are skilled in creating a compelling and mobilizing vision (Bennis 1982;

ORGANIZATIONAL COMPETENCIES

✓ Vision Setting

✓ Management and Supervision

✓ Information and Knowledge Management

✓ Technological Capability

✓ Empowerment and Supportiveness

✓ Teaching and Coaching

✓ Facilitation and Negotiation

Bennis and Nanus 1985; DePree 1993, 26; Luke 1998, 27; Roser, Johnsrud, and Heck 2003; Kouzes and Posner 1995, 91–147). "Show me a leader without vision, and I'll show you someone who isn't going anywhere" (Maxwell 1999, 150). Collins (2001, 95–96) points to three key questions for establishing a vision:

• What can we be the best in the world at doing?

• What drives the economic engine of the organization?

• What is a leader deeply passionate about?

Beyond a focus on the organization and leader, attention to the needs and perspectives of potential followers is also vital in vision setting. In this respect, establishment of a vision consists of "developing a shared sense of destiny" and a "shared sense of purpose" (Kouzes and Posner 1995, 123–33). Successful leaders do this by expressing common values and goals that excite and motivate followers (Berlew 1974; Kanter 2001, 264–67).

Management and Supervision

In many instances, the responsibilities that fall to a leader include tasks that involve management and supervision. Planning is one of them (Reeves 2002a, 99–111; Tromp and Ruben 2004); some others are hiring and reviewing personnel; developing and managing governance systems (Kennedy and Moore 2003, 193–240); forming and managing teams and work groups (Luke 1998, 67; Sorcher and Brant 2002); defining organizational structures and delegating responsibility (Roser, Johnsrud, and Heck 2003). Other management and supervisory responsibilities include improving and reengineering work processes (Brue 2002) and providing appropriate day-to-day oversight of organizational activities.

Relevant in this connection is the cautionary note of Pfeffer and Sutton, who warn of the dangers of overscrutinizing and micromanaging—practices that can detract from performance and innovation (2000, 96).

Information and Knowledge Management

Competency by leaders in managing information and knowledge has gotten increasing attention in recent years (DuBrin 2004, 401–9; Kouzes and Posner 1995, 161–62; Roser, Johnsrud, and Heck 2003). Most fundamentally, the challenge facing leaders is that of creating, within their group or organization, a culture that values and promotes information sharing, collaboration, and learning (Fullan 2001; Kouzes and Posner 1995; Kennedy and Moore 2003, 151–70).

More specifically, leaders need to effectively share, sort, and filter information within groups, organizations, or communities (Wenger, 1998; Pfeffer and Sutton 2000). The objective is to give people as much useful information as possible about what will happen to them and when it will happen; give people detailed information about why actions, especially actions that upset and harm them, were taken; give people as much influence as possible over what happens, when things happen, and the way things happen to them; let people make as many decisions about their own fate as possible; and convey sympathy and concern for disruption, emotional distress, and financial burdens that people face (Pfeffer and Sutton 2000, 136).

But information management is not solely about disseminating information; it's also about two-way communication and engagement. In that respect, it involves the knowledge and skills necessary to engage and use the experience and expertise of relevant stakeholders and "knowledgeholders" (Luke 1998, 70, 107–9).

Technological Capability

Contemporary leaders need an understanding and knowledge of how to best use available technologies to support organizational and leadership effectiveness (Connaughton and Ruben 2004; Connaughton and Daly 2003; 2004). This capability is increasingly important because "geographic interconnects are blurring historical distinctions between what is 'global' and what is 'local'" (Luke 1998, 9).

Operationally, the critical issue is knowing when and how to use technology to support the leadership of teams composed of geographically dispersed people (Majchrzak et al. 2004) and to take advantage of the potentials of "E-Culture" (Kanter 2001, 6).

Empowerment and Supportiveness

Empowerment and supportiveness are frequently mentioned as essential facets of organizational leadership (Bennis 1982; DuBrin 2004, 33, 200–205, 375–79; Komives, Lucas, and McMahon 1998, 80–82; Kouzes and Posner 1995, 151–205, 198–200). Simply stated, the goal of empowerment and supportiveness is enabling others to act (Kouzes and Posner 1995).

Leadership strategies to achieve that goal include encouraging and recognizing the contributions of others (Kanter 2001, 279–80; Kouzes and Posner 1995, 269–313; DePree 1993, 107); helping to enhance the visibility of others and stimulating others' thinking (DePree 1993); enhancing enthusiasm about projects and assignments; and, more generally, facilitating the development of others' talents (Conger 1992, 131; DePree 1993).

On support and recognition, Charles Schwab comments, "I have yet to find the man, however exalted his station, who did not do better work and put forth greater effort under a spirit of approval than under a spirit of criticism" (Maxwell 1999, 8). DePree says leaders should ask themselves a very simple yet basic question: "When was the last time I called to say thank you?" (1993, 119).

Teaching and Coaching

Although it might come as a surprise to some, a number of authors talk about teaching and coaching as leadership competencies (Benton 1998, 187–203; DuBrin 2004, 314–17; Tichy 1997; Reeves 2002b). Reeves goes so far as to suggest that "teaching is the most important job of every leader" (2002b, 59).

Tichy values teaching and learning moments for leaders: "[All excellent leaders] have their own style, but the common denominator is [that] they invest time and emotional energy in teaching and expect all other leaders to do the same thing. Teaching is a way of life for them" (1997, 4).

Leaders are teachers, and they accomplish their goals through the people they teach. Emphasizing the point, Kouzes and Posner note that outstanding leaders are adept at "seizing opportunities to teach" (1995, 223–25). Others use the term "mentoring" to characterize the teaching-coaching role of leaders (Crutcher 2004).

Copyright 2005 by Randy Glasbergen.
www.glasbergen.com

"We're looking for someone who isn't afraid
to fire people. You may be overqualified."

Many other authors, as well, see developing (future) leaders as an important leadership competency (Conger and Benjamin 1999, 251; Collins 2001, 25; Kennedy and Moore 2003, 172–92; Reeves 2002b, 59, 72–74). Through their teaching, leaders play an active role in the development of others' leadership capabilities (Tichy 1997, 41).

Facilitation and Negotiation

Contemporary leaders must be adept negotiators and facilitators (Du-Brin 2004, 14; Hackman and Johnson 2000, 181–82). "Leaders build bridges" (Hasselbein 1999, vii). This may involve facilitating shared leadership (Pearce and Conger 2003); finding common group goals (Kouzes and Posner 1995); and helping others clarify their values and deal effectively with their problems. Heifetz describes it this way: A leader's role "consists of helping people solve the problems for which [the leader] has expertise" (1994, 4–5). The goal is to increase others' adaptive capacity—their ability to clarify values and make progress on the problems those values define.

Negotiation, in the technical and in the more general sense, is a part of organizational life for most leaders. Whether the task involves discussing vacation schedules or salary increases with office staff or developing a contractual relationship between management and various unions, the knowledge and skill associated with strategic negotiation are indispensable. Conflict resolution is a critical facet of negotiation, one that is particularly crucial for contemporary leaders (Deutsch & Coleman, 2000; Mnookin, Ross, & Arrow, 1995).

Positional Competencies

Each of the previous four categories focuses on competencies that are generic in nature. That is, they are described by authors as essential components of leadership across individuals, situations, sectors, and settings.

Yet a number of critical leadership capabilities are specific rather than general—specific to particular sectors, careers, or jobs (Ruben 2004, 64–94). Predictably, little is said about sector-, organization-, or job-specific competencies in the general academic, professional, or popular leadership literature. Nonetheless, we can identify general positional themes that are important. Such themes include *education; experience; expertise; knowledge of a sector and organization; familiarity with task type;* and *language and vocabulary*. Each has both a knowledge and skill component.

POSITIONAL COMPETENCIES

- ✓ Education
- ✓ Experience
- ✓ Expertise
- ✓ Knowledge of Sector
- ✓ Knowledge of Organization
- ✓ Familiarity with Task Type
- ✓ Language and Vocabulary

Education

The value of formal education and certification have long been regarded as important in preparing for leadership roles in organizations (Stogdill 1948). Relevant educational experiences may focus broadly on liberal arts, professional subject matter, or narrower technical content areas (Ruben 2004; Tichy 1997). Having the knowledge that derives from educational accomplishments has substantive value in its own right, providing breadth of perspective and skills that are important in the development of leaders, but the ability to effectively apply that knowledge as a leader is equally vital. Formal education can also be important in some settings for establishing one's credibility.

In addition to formal education—leadership development programs, externships, internships, and other formalized professional enhancement opportunities are among the experiences that contribute to the educational knowledge and skill-set of leaders.

Experience

The idea that "there's no substitute for experience" is a familiar one in discussions of occupational qualifications. On-the-job experience in a particular sector, organization, or position is a recognized asset for leadership. Experience is important—in fact and in perception. That is to say, in addition to the knowledge and skill leaders gain from experience, there is also a symbolic function served by "having experience" that can increase one's credibility in the perceptions of others. Relevant sources of experience may be internships, apprenticeships, or hands-on working experience (Kouzes and Posner 1995).

Expertise

Actual and perceived expertise in areas that are central to the work of a group or organization provides an additional asset for leadership effectiveness (DuBrin 2004, 52).

Whereas education and experience emphasize one's preparation, expertise focuses more on the acquired relevant technical and/or managerial knowledge and skill that an individual has and can demonstrate (Kouzes and Posner 1995, 184). As with other positional competencies, expertise contributes to the substantive knowledge and skill a person brings to leadership roles, as well as having the potential to contribute in positive ways to the perceptions others have of the leader.

"My presentation lacks power and it has no point.
I assumed the software would take care of that!"

As with a working knowledge of sector issues, a strategic understanding of a specific organization can be vital for successful leadership (Kennedy and Moore 2003). Knowledge of a broad array of factors is relevant, including the organization's mission, products and services, aspirations, values, financial standing, culture, history, and present structure (Spear 2004; Kennedy and Moore 2003). Also valuable is a familiarity with organizational strengths, weaknesses, opportunities, and threats (DuBrin 2004, 407–9). Ultimately, the key organizational insights for effective leadership have to do with knowing what's right for the enterprise (Drucker 2004).

Familiarity with Task Type

Aside from their knowledge of a sector and an organization, leaders benefit from familiarity with specific leadership duties or tasks associated with their position (DuBrin 2004, 51; Kirkpatrick and Locke 1991). It is advantageous to have a working familiarity with the managerial or technical tasks performed by others in the organization, particularly those whom a leader supervises. As noted previously, such familiarity can be useful to a leader in actuality and symbolically.

Language and Vocabulary

Being literate in the language of a sector, an organization, a job, or a task type can be extremely helpful. Knowledge of the technical, professional, or managerial vocabulary allows one to converse comfortably about work issues, challenges, and opportunities. Beneficial competencies in this area include fluency relative to key technical and organizational terms, and sector-specific acronyms, as well as the ability to draw on specific examples, vignettes and more extensive case studies that allow a leader to speak substantively, authoritatively and skillfully with colleagues and the public (Tichy 1997).

FIGURE 3—Competence = Understanding + Skill

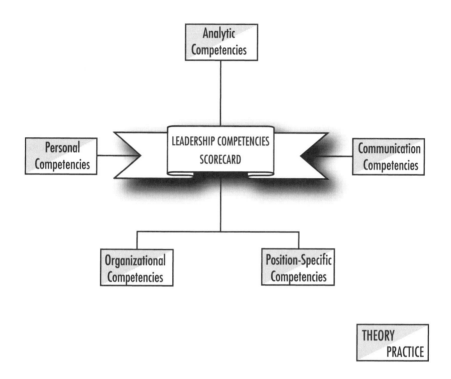

Competency = Understanding + Skill

In the previous pages we have presented the five core competency areas for leaders and discussed seven dimensions associated with each of these areas. The term competency was selected for use in this framework because its meaning is broad enough to include two distinct facets that are important for leadership effectiveness—understanding and skill. As Figure 3 illustrates, each of the competency areas and themes is seen as including an understanding and knowledge of the concepts involved in theory as well as the skill and strategic capability that is required to behave in a manner that is consistent with that understanding, knowledge, or theory.

Whether one thinks of competencies such as self-assessment, conviction and persistence, empowerment and supportiveness, role modeling, or language and vocabulary, an understanding of the concepts involved is certainly crucial. But knowledge alone is insufficient for effective leadership. Indeed, a frequent criticism of formal education is that students become articulate at espousing the theory of various things but often are not able to integrate that understanding effectively in their behavior. Recognizing the potential problems associated with the "knowing-doing gap" (Pfeffer and Sutton 2000) is valuable in many domains, but perhaps in none more so than leadership.

If one possesses only an understanding of a leadership competency and fails to put that knowledge into effective practice, little or no benefit derives from that understanding. To put it more bluntly, unless people are also able to apply their insights in their own behavior—to effectively operationalize their understanding—their knowledge about leadership is wasted.

On the other hand, if someone is skilled in particular areas but does not understand the concepts to which particular behaviors are related, the person has no way to generalize his or her skill and no ability to more broadly and strategically apply those practices in other ways and other settings. Having an inadequate understanding of leadership concepts is as limiting as being ineffective at a skill level. When "natural" skills and behaviors fail to have the desired impact, the lack of a more theoretical understanding greatly restricts one's ability to effectively diagnose the situation and to pursue alternative courses of action. So, while understanding and practical skill are important and valuable in their own right, the goal is to have both, which is to say: Leadership Competency = Understanding + Skill.

The Leadership Competencies Scorecard Inventory

The Leadership Competencies Scorecard Inventory (LCSI) is a tool for use in assessing one's own and others' leadership competencies.

As shown in Figure 4, the LCSI lists and briefly describes each of the 35 competency areas. To the right of the descriptions are blanks for rating one's understanding of the concept and effectiveness in translating that understanding into practice on a 1-to-5 scale.

Scoring instructions accompany the LCSI. Once the scoring and bar charts have been completed, as Figure

5 explains, the results can be quite useful for clarifying one's leadership strengths and weaknesses. Suggestions for using the scoring outcomes include these:

1.   Compare results across the five core competency areas.

2.   Compare results across the 35 competency themes.

3.   Compare results for "understanding" and "effectiveness" across all 35 competency themes.

A copy of the LCSI, along with the Scoring Guide, is provided with this book.

In addition to being interesting in their own right, the results can be extremely useful as the basis for creating a personal leadership development plan. There are a variety of ways in which this could be done. In addition to completing the Inventory for oneself, it can also be useful to have colleagues, family members, or friends complete the "effectiveness" portion of the inventory, to provide an additional perspective on how well you are able to translate your understanding into practice. This can be done in a casual, informal way. Or the process, can be quite structured and formalized such that members of a work group or team systematically—and anonymously—complete the Inventory for one another, with the results being aggregated by a third party and returned to the individuals involved.

Using the LCSI results, it is important to identify areas where improvements are needed, establish several specific personal goals on which to focus, and commit to self-monitoring and periodic progress checks. However one elects to use the results, the completion of the LCSI contributes to the process of self-assessment, which is so essential for leadership development.

Leadership Competencies Scorecard Inventory (LCSI)

Analytic Competencies		Understanding of the Concept					Effectiveness of Your Skills				
Self-Assessment	Analyzing one's own thoughts, emotions, and reactions	1	2	3	4	5	1	2	3	4	5
Problem-Definition	Identifying underlying issues, concerns, problems, and tasks that need to be addressed in a given situation	1	2	3	4	5	1	2	3	4	5
Stakeholder Analysis	Assessing perspectives of those likely to be affected by the decisions, policies, or practices of a leader or organization	1	2	3	4	5	1	2	3	4	5
Systems/Organizational Analysis	Focusing on "the big picture," including short- and long-term concerns and outcomes, for all those affected by leadership decisions, policies, or practices	1	2	3	4	5	1	2	3	4	5
Analysis of Technology to Support Leadership	Assessing available technologies, and their potential strengths and weaknesses for supporting leadership efforts	1	2	3	4	5	1	2	3	4	5
Problem-Solving	Analyzing a situation, identifying possible/appropriate leadership styles and courses of action; ensuring follow through	1	2	3	4	5	1	2	3	4	5
Review and Analysis of Results	Debriefing and analyzing outcomes to derive "lessons learned" that can be applied in a future situation	1	2	3	4	5	1	2	3	4	5
Subtotals—Analytic Competencies											

Leadership Competencies Scorecard Inventory (LCSI)

Personal Competencies		Understanding of the Concept					Effectiveness of Your Skills				
Character, Personal Values, and Ethics	Maintaining personal and professional standards	1	2	3	4	5	1	2	3	4	5
Cognitive Ability and Creativity	Demonstrating insight and imagination	1	2	3	4	5	1	2	3	4	5
Enthusiasm	Maintaining a positive attitude	1	2	3	4	5	1	2	3	4	5
High Standards	Expecting excellent performance from oneself and others	1	2	3	4	5	1	2	3	4	5
Personal Conviction and Persistence	Being dedicated and persevering	1	2	3	4	5	1	2	3	4	5
Self-Discipline and Self-Confidence	Having self-control, focus, and confidence in one's capabilities	1	2	3	4	5	1	2	3	4	5
Tolerance for Uncertainty and Risk-Taking	Maintaining composure and flexibility in the face of change and uncertainty	1	2	3	4	5	1	2	3	4	5
Subtotals—Personal Competencies											

Leadership Competencies Scorecard Inventory (LCSI)

Communication Competencies		Understanding of the Concept					Effectiveness of Your Skills				
Credibility and Charisma	Being admired, seen as magnetic, authoritative, honest, competent, and trustworthy	1	2	3	4	5	1	2	3	4	5
Influence and Persuasion	Convincing others to adopt advocated ideas, points-of-view, or behaviors	1	2	3	4	5	1	2	3	4	5
Interpersonal and Group Orientation	Working effectively in one-on-one and in group settings, including teamwork and group problem-solving.	1	2	3	4	5	1	2	3	4	5
Listening, Attention, Question-Asking, and Learning	Attending verbally and visually to the thoughts, behaviors, and actions of others	1	2	3	4	5	1	2	3	4	5
Public Speaking, Presentation Skills, Debate, and Discussion	Presenting information effectively in a public setting	1	2	3	4	5	1	2	3	4	5
Diversity and Intercultural Orientation	Valuing and working effectively with both men and women, and individuals of varying cultural, racial, ethnic, political, or life-style orientations	1	2	3	4	5	1	2	3	4	5
Role Modeling	Practicing the values and behaviors that one advocates for others	1	2	3	4	5	1	2	3	4	5
Subtotals—Communication Competencies											

Leadership Competencies Scorecard Inventory (LCSI)

Organizational Competencies		Understanding of the Concept					Effectiveness of Your Skills				
Vision-Setting	Motivating and providing a sense of purpose and direction	1	2	3	4	5	1	2	3	4	5
Management and Supervision	Overseeing day-to-day operations, including finances, physical resources, and personnel	1	2	3	4	5	1	2	3	4	5
Information and Knowledge Management	Facilitating the sharing of information within a group or organization	1	2	3	4	5	1	2	3	4	5
Technological Capability	Using appropriate communication technology and media to support leadership initiatives	1	2	3	4	5	1	2	3	4	5
Empowerment and Supportiveness	Enabling others to assume increasing responsibility; encouraging, acknowledging, and reinforcing positive contributions	1	2	3	4	5	1	2	3	4	5
Teaching and Coaching	Encouraging the development of leaders and leadership capacity	1	2	3	4	5	1	2	3	4	5
Facilitation and Negotiation	Encouraging engagement and compromise; conflict management	1	2	3	4	5	1	2	3	4	5
Subtotals—Organizational Competencies											

Leadership Competencies Scorecard Inventory (LCSI)

Positional Competencies		Understanding of the Concept					Effectiveness of Your Skills				
Education	Having relevant formal education and/or training in sector-related competencies	1	2	3	4	5	1	2	3	4	5
Experience	Having prior relevant experience in the sector—e.g., business, healthcare, government, or education	1	2	3	4	5	1	2	3	4	5
Expertise	Having appropriate and/or required job competencies	1	2	3	4	5	1	2	3	4	5
Knowledge of Sector	Understanding the sector, its issues, challenges, and opportunities—e.g., business, healthcare, government, or education	1	2	3	4	5	1	2	3	4	5
Knowledge of Organization	Understanding the particular organization, its issues, challenges, and opportunities	1	2	3	4	5	1	2	3	4	5
Familiarity with Task Type	Knowing about and being comfortable with tasks or work activities that are specific to the sector and organization	1	2	3	4	5	1	2	3	4	5
Language and Vocabulary	Understanding the vocabulary of the sector and organization	1	2	3	4	5	1	2	3	4	5
	Subtotals—Position-Specific Competencies										

Leadership Competencies Scorecard Inventory (LCSI)

Scoring Instructions

Add up the total points in each category (related to both your **understanding of the concept** and **effectiveness of your skills**), and place the subtotals in the appropriate boxes below the respective category.

Transfer your subtotal scores to the blank bar graph below by drawing a horizontal line at the level which corresponds to your particular score. Then, color in the area **below each score line** to create your individual LCS understanding and effectiveness bar charts for each of the five competency areas.

SCALE	Analytic Competencies		Personal Competencies		Communication Competencies		Organizational Competencies		Positional Competencies	
35										
30										
25										
20										
15										
10										
5										
	Understanding	Effectiveness	Understanding	Effectiveness	Understanding	Effectiveness	Understanding	Effectiveness	Understanding	Effectiveness

chapter 9

Reflective Practice:
Understanding ⟷ Skills

At any point in time, some of us have greater proficiency with particular facets of leadership than others. But no matter how knowledgeable or skilled we are, there's always room for improvement.

A virtue of the term competency, as distinct from such terms as ability or aptitude, is that it conveys the idea of "learn-ability." Ability or, and especially, aptitude may connote a talent that is natural or innate, suggesting that either one has it—in which case one is "blessed with a special gift"—or one doesn't, in which case the individual is destined to perpetual inadequacy in a particular area. Competencies, however, can be learned, and our knowledge and skills relative to them can be refined over time.

In the ideal circumstance, the understanding and skills are recipro-cally related. Each has the potential to enhance the other, as captured by the expression "Understanding ⟷ Skills." Reflective practice is the key to making this happen. Simply put, reflective practice involves a commitment to consciously monitor and review one's actions as a leader, the understandings that guided those actions, and the outcomes that result.

The final step in the review process is to refine one's understandings and one's skills as appropriate, based on an analysis of the results. In effect, the commitment is to apply the scientific method to one's own life as a leader—to become, in effect, a leadership researcher—where the focus of study is one's own understanding and behavior, and the outcomes that result.

Committing to reflective practice implies that time will be spent debriefing at the end of interactions, meetings, or events—that is, re-thinking the leadership concepts that guided our actions, reexamining the way those understandings were put into practice, and reflecting on the outcomes. The following are some key questions to use in the reflective process:

- What was I trying to accomplish?
- What understandings—theories or concepts—guided my actions?
- How effective was I at translating my understanding into practice?
- Was the outcome what I expected or hoped for?
- If not, why not?
- What options should I have considered?
- What refinements should I consider for the future in my understanding and my actions?

None of the foregoing is meant to imply that changing one's understanding, and especially one's ability to operationalize that un-derstanding, is a simple matter. Clearly it is not. Nor is it something one does solely on his or her own. But with dedication and the benefit of insight from others, we are all capable of making changes of various kinds, and we do so every day. What's the alternative? Resigning oneself to a view that it is impossible to change, to improve? For most people who aspire to leadership roles—and probably for most people who are bothering to read a book such as this—simply accepting the status quo is not an option.

The most proactive and constructive approach to enhancing leadership competency is much the same as it would be for improving one's musical or athletic competency: continue the commitment to further development and to broadening one's knowledge and skills; devote serious attention to reflective practice; look for opportunities and helpful tools (such as the Leadership Competencies Scorecard Inventory) to aid in genuine self-reflection; solicit other's evaluations and improvement suggestions; identify and learn from others who possess the desired knowledge and skills; look for opportunities to practice and improve; and stay the course!

chapter 10

Using the Leadership Competencies Framework and Scorecard Inventory for Program Planning, Development, and Evaluation

Beyond their helpfulness for personal and professional development of one's own leadership competencies, the framework and scorecard—and this book, more generally—can be useful in the planning, development, or evaluation of leadership courses and programs.

At the most basic level, the framework supplies a list of topics that one could include in the design of educational programming. The "References and Suggested Readings" offers a set of supporting resources. In addition to including information on the competency areas, one could provide experiential activities designed to heighten practical skills and the ability to apply one's understanding in those areas.

Program Evaluation

One can use the framework and scorecard as an inventory for evaluating existing workshops, courses, or programs. They can be used to assess the scope of coverage of the offerings, evaluate the balance in emphasis between knowledge and practical skills, and identify topics and skills that may be important but may not be fully or appropriately addressed in current programming.

Pre- and Post-Test Goal Setting and Assessment

Finally, one can use the scorecard and framework in an assessment mode to help persons or groups clarify current strengths and/or establish improvement targets prior to participating in a workshop, course, or program. From an evaluative perspective, by completing the Leadership Competencies Scorecard Inventory beforehand and afterward, individuals or groups can assess gains in knowledge and skill as a consequence of participation in particular educational experiences.

chapter 11

A Final Note

It can, of course, be argued that the choices of the particular leadership sources reviewed here, and the competency areas that were developed are subjective.

Another researcher might choose different sources, thematic labels, or categorization schemes. Further work adding additional sources would broaden the scope of the framework and further refine the model, and one would hope this project would stimulate further developments of this kind. That said, in its current form, the Competencies Scorecard offers an innovative, practical, and literature-based framework to help students of leadership, program evaluators, and program designers. It can be most helpful to anyone struggling to navigate the complex terrain that is the vast, growing, and diverse professional literature of leadership.

Adair, J. 1983. *Effective Leadership*. Hampshire, England: Gower.

Badaracco, J. L. 2001. "We Don't Need Another Hero." *Harvard Business Review*, September, 121–126.

Barrett, R. 1998. *Liberating the Corporate Soul*. Boston: Butterworth-Heinemann.

Bass, B. M. 1990a. "From Transactional to Transformational Leadership: Learning to Share the Vision." *Organizational Dynamics* 18: 19–31.

Bass, B. M. 1990b. *Leadership, Psychology, and Organizational Behavior*. New York: Harper and Row.

Bass, B. M, and B. J. Avolio. 1990. "The Implications of Transactional and Transformational Leadership for Individual, Team, and Organizational Development." *Research in Organizational Change and Development* 4: 231–272.

Benfari, R. C. 1999. *Understanding and Changing Your Management Style*. San Francisco: Jossey-Bass.

Bennis, W. 1982. "The Artform of Leadership." *Training and Development*, April, 44–46.

Bennis, W. 1989. *On Becoming a Leader*. Reading, Mass.: Addison-Wesley.

Bennis, W. 1999. *Old Dogs. New Tricks*. Provo, Utah: Executive Excellence.

Bennis, W. 2002. "Becoming a Tomorrow Leader." In *Focus on Leadership: Servant-Leadership for the Twenty-first Century*, ed. L. C. Spears and M. Lawrence. New York: Wiley.

Bennis, W., and B. Nanus. 1985. *Leaders: The Strategies for Taking Charge*. New York: Harper and Row.

Benton, D. A. 1998. *Secrets of a CEO Coach*. New York: McGraw-Hill.

Berlew, D. E. 1974. "Leadership and Organizational Excitement." *California Management Review* 17: 21–30.

Bolman, L. G., and T. E. Deal. 1997. *Reframing Organizations.* 2nd ed. San Francisco: Jossey-Bass.

Bonabeau, E. 2004. "The Perils of the Imitation Age." *Harvard Business Review,* June, 45–52.

Brue, G. 2002. *Six Sigma for Managers.* New York: McGraw-Hill.

Brumbeck, W. L., and W. S. Howell. 1976. *Persuasion: A Means of Social Influence.* 2nd ed. Englewood Cliffs, N.J.: Prentice Hall.

Burns, J. M. 1978. *Leadership.* New York: HarperCollins.

Collins, J. C. 2001. *Good to Great.* New York: HarperCollins.

Collins, J.C., and J. I. Porras. 1997. *Built to Last.* New York: HarperCollins.

Conger, J. A. 1992. *Learning to Lead.* San Francisco: Jossey-Bass.

Conger, J. A., and B. Benjamin. 1999. *Building Leaders.* San Francisco: Jossey-Bass.

Conger, J. A., G. M. Spreitzer, and E. E. Lawler III. 1999. *Leader's Change Handbook.* San Francisco: Jossey-Bass.

Connaughton, S. L., and J. A. Daly. 2003. "Long Distance Leadership: Communicative Strategies for Leading Virtual Teams." In *Virtual Teams: Projects, Protocols, and Processes,* ed. D. J. Pauleen, 116–144. Hershey, Pa.: Idea Group.

Connaughton, S. L., and J. A. Daly. 2004. "Leading from Afar: Strategies for Effectively Leading Virtual Teams." In *Virtual and Collaborative Teams: Process, Technologies, and Practice,* ed. S. Godar and S. P. Ferris, 49–75. Hershey, Pa.: Idea Group.

Connaughton, S. L., F. L. Lawrence, and B. D. Ruben. (Sept/Oct 2003) "Leadership Development as a Systematic and Multidisciplinary Enterprise." *Journal of Education for Business* 79 (1): 46–51.

Connaughton, S. L., and B. D. Ruben. 2004. "Millennium Leadership Inc.: A Case Study of Computer and Internet-Based Communication in a Simulated Organization." In *Internet-Based Workplace Communications: Industry and Academic Applications,* ed. K. St. Amant and P. Zemliansky, 40–67. Hershey, Pa: Information Science.

Covey, S. R. 2002. "Servant-Leadership and Community Leadership in the Twenty-first Century." In *Focus on Leadership: Servant-Leadership for the Twenty-first Century*, ed. L. C. Spears and M. Lawrence. New York: Wiley.

Covey, S. R. 2004. *The 8th Habit: From Effectiveness to Greatness*. New York: Free Press.

Crutcher, R. A. 2004. "An Ear for Leadership." *Chronicle of Higher Education*, December 17, B5.

DePree, M. 1993. *Leadership Jazz*. New York: Dell.

DePree, M. 1999. "My Mentors' Leadership Lessons." In *Leader to Leader*, ed. F. Hasselbein and P. M. Cohen, 15–24. San Francisco: Jossey-Bass.

DePree, M. 2002. "Servant-Leadership: Three Things Necessary." In *Focus on Leadership: Servant-Leadership for the Twenty-first Century*, ed. L. C. Spears and M. Lawrence. New York: Wiley.

Deutsch, M. and P. T. Coleman. 2000. *The Handbook of Conflict Resolution: Theory and Practice*. New York.

Drucker, P. F. 1999. "The Shape of Things to Come." In *Leader to Leader*, ed. F. Hasselbein and P.M. Cohen. San Francisco: Jossey-Bass.

Drucker, P. F. 2004. "What Makes an Effective Executive?" *Harvard Business Review*, June, 58–63.

DuBrin, A. W. 2004. *Leadership*. New York: Houghton Mifflin.

Fairhurst, G., and R. A. Sarr. 1996. *The Art of Framing*. San Francisco: Jossey-Bass.

Fiedler, F. E. 1967. *A Theory of Leadership Effectiveness*. New York: McGraw-Hill.

Fine, D. 2005. *The Fine Art of Small Talk*. New York: Hyperion Books.

Fontana, D. 1990. *Social Skills at Work*. New York: Routledge.

Fullan, M. 2001. *Leading in a Culture of Change*. San Francisco: Jossey-Bass.

Gardner, J. 1968. *No Easy Victories*. New York: HarperCollins.

Goffman, E. 1959. *The Presentation of Self in Everyday Life*. Garden City, N.Y.: Doubleday.

Goleman, D. 1998. "What Makes a Leader?" *Harvard Business Review*, November/December, 92–102.

Goleman, D. 2002. *Primal Leadership*. Boston: Harvard Business School Press.

Goodwin, D. K. 1999. "Ten Lessons from Presidents." *In Leader to Leader*, ed. F. Hasselbein and P. M. Cohen, 25–42. San Francisco: Jossey-Bass.

Greenleaf, R. K. 1977. *Servant Leadership*. Mahwah, N.J.: Paulist Press.

Greenleaf, R. K. 2002. "Essentials of Servant-Leadership." In *Focus on Leadership: Servant-Leadership for the Twenty-first Century*, ed. L. C. Spears and M. Lawrence. New York: Wiley.

Grint, K. 2000. *The Arts of Leadership*. Oxford, England: Oxford University Press.

Hackman, M. Z., and C. E. Johnson. 2000. *Leadership*. 3rd ed. Prospect Heights, Ill.: Waveland.

Handy, C. 1993. *Understanding Organizations*. New York: Oxford University Press.

Hargie, O., C. Saunders, and D. Dickson. 1994. *Social Skills in Interpersonal Communication*. 3rd ed. New York: Routledge.

Hasselbein, F. 1999. *Introduction in Leader to Leader*, ed. F. Hasselbein and P. M. Cohen, xi–xiv. San Francisco: Jossey-Bass.

Heifetz, R. A. 1994. *Leadership without Easy Answers*. Cambridge, Mass.: Belknap/Harvard.

Heifetz, R. A., and M. Linsky. 2002. *Leadership on the Line*. Boston: Harvard Business School Press.

Hersey, P. 1984. *The Situational Leader*. Escondido, Calif.: Center for Leadership Studies.

Hersey, P., and K. H. Blanchard. 1979. "Life-Cycle Theory of Leadership." *Training and Development Journal*, June, 94–100.

Hewertson, R. B. 2002. *How to Build a Space Station.* Philadelphia: Xlibris.

Hofstede, G. 1993. "Cultural Constraints in Management Theories." *Academy of Management Executive* 7 (February): 81–94.

Kanter, R. M. 2001. *Evolve.* Boston: Harvard Business School Press.

Kaplan, R. S., and D. P. Norton. 1996. *The Balanced Scorecard.* Boston: Harvard Business School Press.

Kaplan, R. S., and D. P. Norton. 2001. *The Strategy-Focused Organization.* Boston: Harvard Business School Press.

Keegan, J. 1987. *The Mask of Command.* New York: Viking Penguin.

Kelleher, H. 1999. "The Best Lesson in Leadership." In *Leader to Leader,* ed. F. Hasselbein and P. M. Cohen, 43–50. San Francisco: Jossey-Bass.

Kellerman, B. 2004. "Leadership—Warts and All." *Harvard Business Review,* January, 40–44.

Kennedy, K., and M. Moore. 2003. *Going the Distance.* Upper Saddle River, N.J.: Prentice Hall.

Kipnis, D., S.M. Schmidt, C. Swaffin-Smith, and I. Wilkinson. 1984. "Patterns of Managerial Influence: Shotgun Managers, Tacticians, and Bystanders." *Organizational Dynamics* 12 (3): 58–67.

Kirkpatrick, S. A., and E. A. Locke. 1991. "Leadership: Do Traits Matter?" *Academy of Management Executives* 5: 48–60.

Komives, S. R., N. Lucas, and T. R. McMahon. 1998. *Exploring Leadership.* San Francisco: Jossey-Bass.

Kotter, J. P. 1999. *What Leaders Really Do.* Boston: Harvard Business School Press.

Kotter, J. P. 2001. "What Leaders Really Do." *Harvard Business Review,* December, 85–97.

Kouzes, J. M., and B. Z. Posner. 1995. *The Leadership Challenge.* San Francisco: Jossey-Bass.

Kouzes, J. M., and B. Z. Posner. 1996. "Seven Lessons for Leading the Voyage to the Future." In *Leader of the Future,* ed. F. Hasselbein, M. Goldsmith, and R. Beckhard, 99–110. San Francisco: Jossey-Bass.

Luke, J. S. 1998. *Catalytic Leadership.* San Francisco: Jossey-Bass.

Maggio, R. 2005. *The Art of Talking to Anyone.* New York: McGraw-Hill.

Majchrzak, A., A. Malhotra, J. Stamps, and J. Lipnack. 2004. "Can Absence Make a Team Grow Stronger?" *Harvard Business Review,* May, 131–38.

Maxwell, J. C. 1999. *The 21 Indispensable Qualities of a Leader.* Nashville: Thomas Nelson.

McGarvey, R. 2004. "Field Guide to the New CEO." *American Way Magazine,* September 15. Retrieved online at www.americanwaymag.com/business/feature.asp?archive_date=9/15/2004.

Mnookin, R. H., L. Ross, and K. J. Arrow. 1995. *Barriers to Conflict Resolution.* New York: Norton.

Mintzberg, H. 1973. *The Nature of Managerial Work.* New York: Harper and Row.

Mintzberg, H. 1990. "The Manager's Job: Folklore and Fact." *Harvard Business Review,* March/April, 163–76.

Morris, T. 1997. *If Aristotle Ran General Motors.* New York: Owl Books.

Morrison, A. M. 1992. *The New Leaders: Guidelines on Leadership Diversity in America.* San Francisco: Jossey-Bass.

Nadler, D. A., and M. L. Tishman. 1990. "Beyond the Charismatic Leader: Leadership and Organizational Change." *California Management Review* 32 (winter): 77–97.

Northouse, P. 2004. *Leadership.* Thousand Oaks, Calif.: Sage.

Noyes, R. B. 2001. *The Art of Leading Yourself.* Fort Bragg, Calif.: Cypress Press.

Patterson, K., et al. 2002. *Crucial Conversations: Tools for Talking When Stakes are High.* New York: McGraw-Hill.

Pearce, C. L., and J. A. Conger. 2003. *Shared Leadership*. Thousand Oaks, Calif.: Sage.

Pfeffer, J., and R. I. Sutton. 2000. *The Knowing-Doing Gap*. Cambridge, Mass.: Harvard University Business School Press.

Prentice, W. C. H. 2004. "Understanding Leadership." *Harvard Business Review*, January, 102–8.

Prince, H. T., II, et al. 1998. *Leadership in Organization*. Garden City Park, N.Y.: Avery.

Reeves, D. B. 2002a. *The Daily Disciplines of Leadership*. San Francisco: Jossey-Bass.

Reeves, D. B. 2002b. *The Leader's Guide to Standards*. San Francisco: Jossey-Bass.

Roser, V. J., L. K. Johnsrud, and R. H. Heck. 2003. "Academic Deans and Directors: Assessing Their Effectiveness from Individual and Institutional Perspectives." *Journal of Higher Education* 74 (1): 1–25.

Ruben, B. D. 2004. *Pursuing Excellence in Higher Education: Eight Fundamental Principles*. San Francisco: Jossey-Bass.

Ruben, B. D. 2005a. "The Center for Organizational Development and Leadership at Rutgers University: A Case Study, 'Organization Development and Change in Universities.'" A special issue of *Advances in Developing Human Resources* 7 (3): 368–95.

Ruben, B. D. 2005b. *Excellence in Higher Education: An Integrated Guide to Assessment, Planning, and Improvement*. Washington, D.C.: National Association of College and University Business Officers.

Ruben, B. D. 2006. *The Leadership Style Inventory (LSI): Becoming a Strategic Leader*. Washington, D.C.: National Association of College and University Business Officers.

Ruben, B. D., and L. Stewart, 2005. *Communication and Human Behavior*, Fifth Edition. Boston: Allyn-Bacon.

Schein, E. H. 1992. *Organizational Culture and Leadership*. 2nd ed. San Francisco: Jossey-Bass.

Schein, E. H. 1996. "Leadership and Organizational Culture." In *Leader of the Future,* ed. F. Hasselbein, M. Goldsmith, and R. Beckhard, 59–69. San Francisco: Jossey-Bass.

Senge, P. 1990. *The Fifth Discipline.* New York: Doubleday.

Senge, P. 1996. "Leading Learning Organizations." In *Leader of the Future,* ed. F. Hasselbein, M. Goldsmith, and R. Beckhard, 41–57. San Francisco: Jossey-Bass.

Sorcher, M., and J. Brant. 2002. "Are You Picking the Right Leaders?" *Harvard Business Review,* February/March, 78–87.

Spear, S. J. 2004. "Learning to Lead at Toyota." *Harvard Business Review,* May, 78–87.

Spears, L. C., and M. Lawrence. 2002. *Focus on Leadership: Servant-Leadership for the Twenty-first Century.* New York: Wiley.

Stogdill, R. M. 1948. "Personal Factors Associated with Leadership: A Survey of the Literature." *Journal of Psychology* 25: 35–71.

Tichy, N. M. 1997. *The Leadership Engine.* New York: HarperCollins.

Tromp, S. A., and B. D. Ruben. 2004. *Strategic Planning in Higher Education.* Washington, D.C.: National Association of College and University Business Officers.

Useem, M. 1998. *The Leadership Moment.* New York: Random House.

Vroom, V. H., and P. W. Yetton. 1973. *Leadership and Decision-Making.* Pittsburgh: University of Pittsburgh.

Wenger, E. 1998. *Communities of Practice.* Cambridge, England: Cambridge University Press.

Wheatley, M. J. 1999. *Leadership and the New Science.* San Francisco: Berrett-Koehler.

Wheatley, M. 2002. "The Work of the Servant-Leader." In *Focus on Leadership: Servant-Leadership for the Twenty-first Century,* ed. L. C. Spears and M. Lawrence. New York: Wiley.

Witherspoon, P. D. 1997. *Communicating Leadership.* Boston: Allyn and Bacon.

Witherspoon, P. D. 2004. "Communication at the Center of Leadership Education: Looking to the Future." Paper presented at the Annual Conference of the National Communication Association, May. Chicago.

Young, R. L. *Understanding Misunderstandings: A Practical Guide to More Successful Human Interaction.* Austin: University of Texas Press, 1999.

Yukl, G., and J. B. Tracey. 1992. "Consequences of Influence Tactics Used with Subordinates, Peers, and the Boss." *Journal of Applied Psychology*, August, 525–35.

Zaleznik, A. 1992. "Managers and Leaders: Are They Different?" *Harvard Business Review*, March/April, 126–35.